Smudging

Clear Negative Energy From Your Home & Life

Susan K. Edwards

Licensed Spiritual Healer-Coach, Reiki Master, Certified Ho'oponopono Teacher, Advanced Pranic Healing®, Lightworker, Sound Healer, Christian Minister, Psychic Medium, Empath, Author, Facilitator, and Public Speaker

Published by

Susan K. Edwards, dba
Wildhair Studios, LLC
Books that Entertain, Enlighten and Empower
Paducah, KY 42001

Copyright © 2018 by Susan K. Edwards
All rights reserved.

All rights reserved. This book or any portion thereof may not be reproduced or used in any manner whatsoever without the express written permission of the publisher except for the use of brief quotations in a book review.

http://www.NiceRockShop.com
NiceRockShop@gmail.com

ISBN-13: 978-1717313874
ISBN-10: 1717313876

Dedication

I want to thank everyone who has asked me questions about how to smudge and clear negative energy from their homes and lives, and those who have helped me frame the answers to those questions.

Contents

Foreword 1
What is Smudging? 3
Why Clear Stale Energy? 5
How To Clear Stale Energy 7
Residual Energy 9
5 Clear Signs You Need To Clear Negative Energy
.... 11
First Steps 13
Okay, I May Be Part of The Problem 15
What's next? 19
Herbs to Use in Smudging 21
Crystals 23
How to Clear, Charge, and Program Crystals 25
Crystals To Consider 27
Before you Begin 29
Now, Light the Sage or Incense 31
Using Clearing Sprays 35
Clearing Your Space Using Frequencies 37
Using Solfeggio Frequencies 39
Shielding Your Sacred Space from Negative People
and Energy 41
Using Essential Oils 43
Vehicle Protection 47
Protective Grids Around Your Property 49
Blessing Ceremony 51
Maintenance 53
Cautions 55

Foreword

How to Clear Negative Energy From Your Home & Life

This book explores the possible causes of negative energy and provide remedies to remove that negative energy from your home and life.

What is Smudging?

Smudging is a ceremony or procedure to remove negative, or stale energy and influences from a person, place, or object. It is also an effective method for energizing or blessing a person, place, or thing. It has been used for centuries by many different cultures to create sacred spaces.

You may know of the Native American traditions using smudge. There are many resources that focus on the cultural and religious traditions. In this book, however, I'll focus on some simple step-by-step instructions to clear negative energy and create a loving, sacred environment in your home or office. You may choose to make it a spiritual occasion—or not.

Why Clear Stale Energy?

Clearing negative or stale energy brings the frequencies of your surroundings to a higher level and creates a sacred space, promoting a more calm, balanced, and healthy environment. Plus, it just feels better!

Every living thing leaves a plume of energy as it moves through life. Science has discovered we humans can be identified by our individual bioplume. Each one of us is unique, and our plume contains our personal microviruses, microbacteria, sweat, sound (frequencies), and heat. When we—and those around us—are healthy and happy, we leave less stale energy that needs to be cleared. When we are surrounded by stale, negative, chaotic, or dis-eased energy, we can be affected by those subtle frequencies in a negative way.

How To Clear Stale Energy

One method is through resonance. Resonance is when something (in this example, our energy field) starts to vibrate in harmony with, or in sympathy with, something else. For example, a guitar string vibrates alongside of the string next to it, sharing vibrations and frequencies, when the first string is being plucked.

When life around us gets loud, dissonant, or chaotic, we tend to become more loud, dissonant, and chaotic. If you are in a stressful environment, all that dissonance around you can create emotional and physical stress and disease in your life. If you're an empath or a sensitive and particularly in tune with emotional frequencies, you are most likely an energetic "hot mess" most of the time if you don't keep your surroundings clear.

We've all noticed dissonance even if that isn't what you called it. We might say things like, "I don't like their vibes." Or, "They rub me the wrong way."

Residual Energy

We can be affected by the residual energy around us. If that energy is overtly negative, we will start to resonate with those lower frequencies. Here's an example of residual energy.

Imagine a mirror. Touch it and you will leave your fingerprints on the surface. Even if you wipe the fingerprints off, you will still see the heat energy signature of your fingers on the mirror if you use a thermal camera. Though you might not see the fingerprints, you've left some of your energy on the mirror.

After a period of time, that heat signature will fade. Handle the mirror a lot, and you will have a lot of fingerprints and a lot of heat signatures on the mirror. If the energy on your hands was dirty (as in, you were sick) you can expect to find viruses or bacteria and potentially hotter fingerprints left behind.

Taking the mirror analogy further, let's say you come home from a long day at work or school and plop down on your favorite chair. You are leaving energy signatures everywhere and on everything. Sad energy, mad energy, sick energy, happy energy—it all gets left behind on everything and anything you touch.

Then let's say you wanted to use that mirror I mentioned earlier, but it had a lot of fingerprints (energy signatures) all over it. You might clean it off to get a better reflection. That is exactly what you are doing when you clear your space using smudging or a technique with frequencies and vibrations.

5 Clear Signs You Need To Clear Negative Energy

Life is fluid. Everyone experiences the ebb and flow of being human with everyday highs and lows.

Sometimes relationships start, mature and wither. People get sick, jobs disappear, and disasters can strike. So how do you know if it's just life, or if you are being affected by something more, like negative energy? Here are five clear signs your problem may be energetic in nature.

1. You are constantly sick for no apparent reason and none of your doctors can give you a solid diagnosis. It may be time to explore the energy around you.

2. You are experiencing "free floating anxiety." Again, there is no obvious reason for your anxiety and yet you are experiencing some level of panic attacks.

3. You are constantly feeling "drained." You're tired beyond what would be normal for your level of activity.

4. You're at odds with everyone, your friends, family, and co-workers—constantly.

5. Nothing, and I mean nothing, is going right. Your world is literally crumbling around you, through no fault of your own.

Okay, so you've clicked off one or more of the five boxes. Now what?

First, take a deep breath. All of us have stress and some level of stale or negative energy in our lives. The trick is to recognize it and know how to clear it before it becomes problematic. The good news is you can clear it with some simple, effective methods.

Please note if you are getting sick, be sure to rule out all the usual suspects and see a medical and or mental health professional. Make sure your home doesn't have a mold issue, or other environmental hazard that is causing the illness.

First Steps

Take an Honest Assessment

If you need to improve your lifestyle, add something, anything to your clearing and blessing ritual that starts to overcome whatever is polluting your life. Intention is powerful. Have the intention to take better care of yourself.

If necessary, clean up your lifestyle. Make sure you are eating right, exercising, sleeping well, and managing your stress. Any addictions or self-destructive behaviors like over- or under-eating, smoking, drugs, or alcohol are open invitations to stale and negative energies, and worse, entities. Addressing your lifestyle issues will exponentially improve the effectiveness of these energetic clearing techniques.

With that said, here are some simple things you can do to clear up stale energy and get things flowing in a positive direction.

First, most clients tell me, they will be happy and more positive when things start to go right, and their situation improves. They are always resistant when I explain they have it backwards. Things will improve in their lives and they will be happier when they get and stay positive. This is often the most challenging part of their change, but it is the critical adjustment that will ensure success.

"Yeah, yeah. I thought this book was about clearing my house of negativity. What's all this hooey about my lifestyle and positive attitude?"

Great question!

Let's say I had a client that wanted me to help them figure out why their hardwood floors were constantly getting scratched. I spent a little time observing and noticed everyone in the family wore metal spikes on their shoes. They could refinish their floors as often as they liked, but until they changed their habit of wearing spiked shoes, the problem would remain. That's why we're talking about your lifestyle. You can smudge and clear all you want, but if YOU are one of the sources of the negativity, let's fix the problem, not just treat the symptoms.

Okay, I May Be Part of The Problem

What Do I Do?

First, stop gossiping and criticizing everyone—whether you feel they deserve it or not—STOP! Right now. Mom offered good advice, "If you can't say something nice, don't say anything at all."

No more complaining about your job—school—husband—wife—lover—brother—sister—children—neighbors. You get the point. Stop gripping! Oh, boy, that's a tough one for some people.

Take a long, hard, and honest look at your relationships. Do some or most of them consist of extensive negative banter? Are you constantly swapping stories, complaints, and gossip about everyone, anyone and everything?

STOP! Energetically, you are creating, reinforcing, and spreading dissonance. Dissonance sets the stage for negativity, and negativity opens the door to all manner of particularly unpleasant situations and entities.

When you spend time either listening to, or talking about, negative situations and people in your life, it's like backing up the garbage truck and doing a toxic dump. Whether you are the dumper or the dumpee, either way, all that garbage has to be dealt with at some point and at some level. When you look at it that way, it's much easier to stop the negative talk and gossip than to have to clean up the energetic garbage later.

Be forewarned—situations, jobs, and relationships founded on the principle of dissonance will likely wither and disappear once you tune into more positivity and harmony. This is often an exceptionally good thing. But it can be startling when these transformations happen quickly.

Be gentle with yourself. This can be an enormous change and may take some time and practice. But keep working at improving your communications. Miracles will manifest!

Next

You've stopped talking about everything that is going wrong, how awful life is, and how bad you feel. Start talking about what is going right (however minuscule it might be!) and how much you love feeling good.

Be mindful of your surroundings and what you are allowing into your life. Remove overtly negative items. Don't invite in problems with demonic images, violent or distressing music or artwork.

Reduce or eliminate watching or listening to violent and highly distressing TV shows and movies. Just say NO to violent video games! This is a biggie and most of us blindly allow all this negativity into our homes without questioning the effect it is having on us, our families and our lives. In fact, we often bring it into our lives under the illusion that it is entertainment. Trust me. It is not!

Eliminate or isolate toxic relationships. If you are the one that is toxic, work on yourself. Clean up what needs to be cleaned up. You know what you need to do. I suggest you are reading this because you are ready. You can do whatever personal work necessary to get balanced, happy and healthy. You only need to set your intention to achieve your dreams.

Feel genuine gratitude for everything in your life. Any time you are tempted to talk about what's wrong, pause and find something to say about what's right with the situation or person. And yes, this can take some practice.

What's next?

Okay, that takes care of your personal energetic assignment.

On to the house and office clean up.

Do a physical cleaning. Stale and negative energy can get "stuck" or hide in clutter.

Open windows, and "air" the place out. Visualize bringing in fresh, clean, bright and cheerful energy. Turn on the fan to facilitate moving the old out and bringing in the fresh.

Tools Needed

Next, gather your tools such as smudge, incense, clearing spay, feather or fanning tool, shell, or ashtray to catch ashes. You can also add essential oils, crystals, and or any protection items you choose.

Bundles of herbs for smudging can be acquired in metaphysical stores or online. They can come loose or in small, medium, and large bundles. Even a small bundle will normally be plenty for a medium-sized area. You can reuse the bundle, so if you don't burn it all, you can use it the next time.

Herbs to Use in Smudging

White sage is universally useful for healing and blessing a person, place, or object. It is great for clearing stale energy and unwanted influences around you and creating a sacred space.

Cedar is a known for protection and is great to cleanse a home or apartment when first moving in, inviting unwanted spirits to leave, and protecting a person, place, or object from unwanted influences.

Sweetgrass or Seneca grass (also called holy grass,) and vanilla grass (which has a sweet, vanilla-like scent,) are helpful in bringing the essence of the feminine and the blessing of Mother Earth's love. It also reminds us that the earth provides everything we need.

Lavender is often used to remove negative energy and protect against evil. It calms and harmonizes the mind, restores emotional balance, and can create a peaceful harmonious environment. It also attracts angelic beings. Burning loose lavender is best done on charcoal tablets.

Copal is sacred tree sap from Mexico and is similar to frankincense. It produces a scent that is crisp, clean, sharp, and somewhat citrus-like. Burning copal is best done on charcoal tablets.

Frankincense is a tree resin that can be used to cleanse and protect the soul. Frankincense is important to most major religions in the world and is still found in many of their rituals. Folklore claims that it helps to promote clairvoyance. It can be used for anointing, psychic protection, purification, dispelling of negative and harmful energies, create and purify sacred spaces, and exorcism. Burning frankincense is best done on charcoal tablets.

Myrrh is a tree resin and is said to help one maintain a state of enlightenment. It also helps you see your own truth. Burning myrrh is best done on charcoal tablets.

Palo Santo is also known as a holy tree or holy wood. It is widely used for spiritual purification and energy clearing. It can restore tranquility and calm emotions. It's great for helping create a sacred space.

Crystals

You may choose to add healing or protective crystals to your clearing techniques and ceremonies. The frequencies of the different crystals can help strengthen your aura, keep you focused, and help raise the vibrations in the space you are clearing. They are not required and are completely optional, so don't worry if you don't have any crystals. If you do want to use crystals, they will be more effective if they have been cleared, charged, and programmed. It is simple to do and recommended if you plan on using them during the ceremony.

How to Clear, Charge, and Program Crystals

Clearing Your Crystals

One tried-and-true way to clear crystals is with salt water. Get a container you will not be using later for food and throw in a handful of salt. Any table salt will work. I often get questions from clients if they should use Himalayan pink salt. You can, but plain old, cheap salt will do the trick. Salt has green prana. It's power lies in salt's green frequency and that it is a desiccant, pulling the negativity from the crystals.

Fill the bowl with enough water to completely cover the crystals. Soak them for at least thirty minutes. Rinse them in clear running water if possible. A bowl of fresh water will do. It's important to completely remove all traces of the salt. Rub gently if appropriate, and envision any dirty energy being lifted off and properly disposed of. Gently pat them dry.

Caution: not all gemstones can tolerate salt or water. Check before soaking them.

You can also smudge your crystals. Light your smudge and waft the smoke around your crystals to clear them.

Charging Your Crystals

To charge your crystal, you can hold it as you pray over it. Alternatively, you can set it out in bright sun, an electrical storm, full moon, or bury it in the ground overnight. You will want to mark the spot where you bury it, as more than one crystal has been lost this way!

Program Your Crystal

To program your crystal, hold it and focus your attention on the crystal. Say, "Crystal, listen to me. Strengthen my aura and protect me from psychic contamination." Use whatever simple command you wish your crystal to do for you. If you want all your crystals to do the same thing, you can program them together. If not, work on programming each one individually.

There you go! Your crystals are now cleared, charged, programmed, and ready to help you in your ceremony. You can either use them in your space or hold them while you conduct your smudging.

Crystals To Consider

Obsidian is a powerful protection crystal. It helps clear, strengthen, and protect your aura. It is very strong protection against psychic attacks. Obsidian has a lot of earth energy. It's easily programmed to form a barrier of protection to prevent unwanted energies from entering your space or your aura. Place it in your sacred space, and program it to form a protective shield that prevents anything evil from entering. It's self-cleaning, which is great for setting it and forgetting it!

Black tourmaline is very grounding and one of the most powerful stones for psychic protection and shielding against negative energy.

Rose quartz is known as the stone of love and can help keep your heart chakra open while being protected. It can help you stay loving and prevent you from becoming bitter.

Amethyst is an excellent choice to connect to the Divine, protect your aura and shield you against negativity. It's a master stone and perfect for assisting you in clearing negative energy.

These are some of my favorites, but any of your crystals or talismans can be cleared and programmed to shield you during smudging and during meditation.

Before You Begin

Once you have gathered your tools, and before you begin, say a prayer, and surround yourself and anyone in the house or office with protection. Don't forget to protect your pets. You can use the Lord's Prayer, the prayer of protection, or any prayer or declaration that you prefer. Here's one of my favorites, the Prayer of Protection by James Dillet Freeman:

"The Light of God surrounds me.
The Love of God enfolds me.
The Power of God protects me.
The Presence of God watches over me.
Wherever I am, God is!"

Next

Energy doesn't need an open door or window to leave but it helps your left brain visualize the energy leaving. So, open a window or crack the door, and hold the intention that the stale energy leaves via that opening. If available, turn on any fans to facilitate even better movement of stale energy.

Now, Light the Sage or Incense

Now that you have your smudging tools ready, your crystals placed (optional), and you and your space are clean, you can begin the smudging ceremony. Say a prayer over the items and thank them for helping you clear the stale energy and for creating a sacred space. Light your bundle of sage, smudge, or incense, and allow it to burn for a moment and then extinguish the flame so it begins to smoke. The smoke is what you will be wafting through your space.

Place the smoking bundle with the lit end down in the receptacle with the fireproof sand or salt to catch the ashes. Holding the shell (or ashtray) in one hand and feather in the other, pick a starting point and begin at the bottom right of your designated space. Use caution. There is a hot ember that can start a fire.

You can go clockwise to bring in energy or counterclockwise to get it to leave. As you move through your space, have the intention of filling it with white light, love, and joy. Any of the low vibrations like anger, hate, and despair are not compatible and can't coexist with the higher vibration of love. Your job is to bring the vibrations of your space up to something closer to love.

Here is an example of a statement you may choose to use:

"This is a place of light and love. All who enter are transformed by the power of unconditional God Love! Only light and love may exist in this space."

Next, move to one corner of the wall, and systematically waft the smoke into the corners counter—clockwise around the side, top, down the other side, and across the floor back to your starting point. Use your intention to form a complete grid that goes up and down to each corner of the wall, ceiling, and nooks and crannies.

Once that wall is finished, turn to repeat the grid pattern on each wall of the room. Be sure to go around furniture and large objects in the room. Open cabinets, closet doors, and, using your intention, fan the clearing smoke in and around the closets and cabinets. Don't forget to go around your toilet—it's literally where everyone's "crap" ends up!

Don't neglect to smudge TVs, mirrors, windows, radios or modems. These can all be portals that bring things into your sacred space and should be cleared.

After that room is finished, move to the next room, and be sure to clear the hallways as you move through the house or office.

To clear crawl spaces and attics, open the door if possible, and using your intention, fan the smoke into the air to clear stale energy. It is helpful, but not necessary to enter the area in order to clear it.

If you or someone in your home is allergic to smoke, or it isn't appropriate or convenient to burn smudge, you can use either clearing sprays or vibrations.

The first-time you smudge, or if you haven't smudged for a long time, it will likely take about an hour or so. I keep my house pretty clear energetically, so you can also use sprays and frequencies for quickies that I call a "spot clearing."

Before Clearing

Room, furniture or areas may feel stale, heavy or generally depressive or downright negative.

Suggested Smudging patterns and examples of problem areas to concentrate your clearing

After Clearing

Your area should feel considerably lighter, brighter, fresh and airy. If not, go back and concentrate on the area that still feels heavy.

Using Clearing Sprays

If burning incense or smudge is not practical, you can use a clearing spray. Follow the same steps as if you were going to burn a smudge stick or incense but use a clearing spray instead. A feather or fan is helpful to waft the spray into the corners in the same way you would use it with smoke.

There are several clearing sprays available at stores or online. If you would like to create your own, here are a few recipes I created for a two-oz spray bottle.

Recipe one (my favorite):
- Four drops lavender essential oil
- Pinch of salt
- Fill with (cheapest) vodka
- Shake and use as needed

Recipe two:
- Thirty drops sage essential oil
- Four drops frankincense essential oil
- Pinch of salt

- Fill with holy or blessed water
- Shake and use as needed

Why use vodka? First, it doesn't have a smell, and if I use it to clear energy from my hands, it doesn't dry them out. I will also use it to clear furniture and my bed, and it evaporates quickly and doesn't stain.

Holy water can be purchased from your local Catholic gift store or church, or you can make your own.

A quick Google search will provide you with complete instructions on how to follow Catholic procedures or inspire you on how to create your own ritual to bless the water.

Clearing Your Space Using Frequencies

If you have tuning forks, use them. Most do not, so no problem! You can download the high sacred solfeggio frequency of 963 hertz to your smart phone. Clapping loudly also works. Grab some pots and pans and a wooden spoon and move through the space making noise. You have many choices.

Reclaim your space with statements of authority. An example of what I use is, "This is a place of light and love! Only those from the highest source for my highest good may enter." Act like you mean it! Use your most authoritative voice.

All the noise and clapping will break up stale energy. Your positive intentions along with praying brings in happy, upbeat frequencies. Have the intention of filling the space with light and love.

No, you don't have to do this every time you want to clear your space. How often do you need to do it? Well, it's like dusting your furniture. You just know when it's time.

Using Solfeggio Frequencies

Using sacred solfeggio frequencies is also extremely effective method of resetting your vibrational environment.

What are Solfeggio Frequencies?

According to one of my favorite sites, Attuned Vibrations, "Solfeggio frequencies make up the ancient 6-tone scale thought to have been used in sacred music, including the beautiful and well-known Gregorian Chants. The chants and their special tones were believed to impart spiritual blessings when sung in harmony. Each solfeggio tone is comprised of a frequency required to balance your energy and keep your body, mind and spirit in perfect harmony.

The main six solfeggio frequencies are:

396 Hz – Liberating guilt and fear
417 Hz – Undoing situations and facilitating change
528 Hz – Transformation and miracles (DNA repair)
639 Hz – Connecting/relationships
741 Hz – Expression/solutions
852 Hz – Returning to spiritual order

An internet search for free tones will net several sites where you can download tones to play off your smart phones.

No matter which method you use, once you are confident each area is clear, you can bless it and keep it clear with your prayers of gratitude and protection.

Shielding Your Sacred Space From Negative People and Energy

If you have problems with negative energy or people entering your sacred area, you can further protect your space with a thin line of salt along the threshold of the area. Putting salt, crystals, holy water, or essential oils at the entrance of the room or area is also highly effective in keeping negative energy outside of your sacred spaces.

Obsidian at the thresholds is effective in keeping unwanted things from entering your space. Obsidian is also one of the crystals that releases any stale or negative energy safely and doesn't require clearing on your part. Refer to the section on how to clear, charge, and program your crystal if you plan on using obsidian.

I have obsidian at all my doorways, one on either side of the doorjamb at home and at the store. I have them programmed to form a grid so that anything overtly negative or outright evil cannot come through without being invited.

Sometimes it's uncomfortable and a little unsettling when I have someone who comes to the store door, stops, takes a quick look around, and then leaves. I know that my obsidian is working. When I look at this person, I realize that their vibrations don't match up with what I'm doing and the high vibrations at the Rock Shop.

Once, I was distracted talking and joking around with some regular customers and not paying attention. There was a man that had come into the entrance of the store but stopped at the interior door where the obsidian was placed. He stood there for several moments. Without thinking about it, I said to the man, "Well, come on in."

I immediately knew that I had committed an error! He stepped in the door, and the first thing out of his mouth was, "You really have to be careful about vampires around here now."

The regular customers and I all looked at one another and realized I had invited him in! Oops! My friends and customers in the store at the time happened to be quite familiar with energy work so we were trying to get this guy and his energy out as quickly as possible!

Once he left, we immediately set about smudging the place, clearing, and blessing. And yes, we were singing and clapping and dancing and making declarations.

Believe me, if you have an effective grid, evil can't get in unless you invite it in.

Using Essential Oils

Dispersing Negativity and Creating Your Sacred Space

Essential oils have been used for hundreds of years in countless cultures to help disperse negativity and create sacred spaces. Here are just a few of the oils you could use to help you clear yourself or your space of negative or stale energy. You have the option of using them in a spray, in a diffuser, or anointing yourself, another person, or an object.

Be certain to properly dilute any essential oil before applying it to your skin. You will need some sort of a fatty carrier oil. Even olive oil will serve as a carrier oil in a pinch. Follow the instructions on the label, but generally you don't want a solution stronger than about 10 percent if you are applying it to your skin. Use full strength in a diffuser or if you are anointing something other than a person. You can put a drop or two on your palm, gently rub your hands together once or twice to activate the oil (don't rub too vigorously, a few quick rubs will do the trick). Drag your hands through your aura to clear it and balance your chakras. Take a deep breath of the fragrant oil. Then ceremoniously anoint yourself by rubbing your shoulders or the crown of your head before beginning.

See the previous section for recipes to create a spray. If you are using the oils on your skin or another person, please follow any instructions on the bottle and **use caution if you are pregnant or have any health concerns**.

Here are some of my favorites and how they may help you with clearing ceremonies:

Basil—aura cleansing, purification.

Bay—spiritual cleansing, purification.

Cajeput—purification, cleansing, protection, dispels negative energies.

Cedarwood, Virginian—protection and purification.

Citronella—purification, dispelling negative energy.

Clary sage—protection and psychic clarity.

Eucalyptus—purification, exorcism, banishing negative energies.

Frankincense—Anointing, psychic protection, purification, dispelling of negative and harmful energies, create and purify sacred spaces, exorcism.

Galbanum—purification, protection, banishing negative energies.

Geranium—protection, dispelling apprehension, and negativity.

Grapefruit—to help deal with jealousy, envy, bitterness.

Hyssop—purification, protection, spiritual and aura cleansing.

Lavender—inner peace and purification.

Lemongrass—purification, to clear psychic channels.

Lemon verbena—purification, cleansing of items.

Lime—protection, energy of action, purification.

Juniper—purification, protection, to dispel negative energies and entities.

Myrrh—psychic protection, purification, dispelling of negative and harmful energies.

Niaouli—Purification, protection, release of negative energies that "clog up" the physical and mental bodies, aura cleansing.

Peppermint—purification and dispels negative thought forms.

Pine—purification, dispels negative energy, crystal cleansing, protection.

Sage—aura cleansing, dispels negative energies, purification, protection.

Sandalwood—dispels fears and negative energies.

Tea tree—aura cleansing, protection, purification.

Thyme—purification, protection, inner strength, and emotional courage.

Vetiver—protection, grounding.

Vehicle Protection

You can also smudge your car, property, and outbuildings if you are having issues with negativity or stale energy in those spaces.

I had a customer that was having trouble with some coworkers. She was a little afraid of one of them. So, we took some obsidian, cleansed it, charged it, and programmed it to protect her from evil and she put in her car. She came in the next week to tell me that this coworker had come over to her car and asked her for a ride home. Before she could answer, he opened the car door and started to get in but couldn't. Of course, he did not know that the obsidian was in the car. He couldn't get past her protection.

She said he seemed quite confused, mumbled something, and left quickly. So, it was an extremely effective. She was back for more obsidian to put in her home!

Protective Grids Around Your Property

What if you need to form a protective grid around your home and property? Get some clearing incense sticks, like Frankincense, Sandalwood, or Lavender. Light them and place the burning incense sticks at the four corners of your property. Envision them forming a protective shield around your property. Have the intention of the grid protecting below your home and property as well as above. Make it a complete bubble of protection.

You can further strengthen the protection by taking another stick of burning incense and saying a prayer of protection as you walk to each of the corners of your property.

You can make declarations like, "This grid of protection covers my home, property, buildings, cars, livestock, people, and pets. Nothing negative can get in. Anything negative can get out. Nothing can dissolve or disintegrate this grid except me."

Take a moment and write out your own affirmation. Make it appropriate for your intentions.

You can also use crystals at the corners of your property. Again, clear, charge, and program your crystal, instructing it to form a barrier of protection. Then bury the crystals in the corners of your property. Some crystals to consider would be obsidian, black tourmaline, rose quartz, or amethyst.

Salt is also a choice. We cleared a home where the property had underground water coming from a pond considerably off the property. Some horrible things had happened at that little pond. The negative entities were using this water line as a conduit to enter my client's property. We put salt in the corner of the property where the underground water entered. After much clearing and cleansing, we formed an effective block, but it did need to be refreshed on occasion.

You can find chunks of salt like Himalayan pink salt online, or at certain retail establishments like the Rock Shop.

Blessing Ceremony

Now that your space or object is clear, it's time to do your blessing ceremony. This stabilizes the frequencies and cements your intention to keep the space in high vibration.

Your ceremony should reflect your belief and traditions. There is no right or wrong, as it is personal and unique to you and your family. You can make it as traditional as saying prayers and declaring the space as sacred and holy, or as non-traditional as you choose.

As I move through the space, I declare in no uncertain terms, "This is a place of light and Love! All who enter are transformed by the power of unconditional God Love!" I will clap, sing, and dance my way around the area.

While I do tend to do this by myself, I have included others. And yes, it's always a little uncomfortable to get started. This isn't normally how we act! But trust me when I say this is extremely effective in claiming or reclaiming your space, and even your life.

Push through. Remember, your true audience is the spirit world, not the human world. If you come off as tentative and weak, well, a strong negative entity isn't going to take you very seriously. Act like you own the place! Oh. Wait. You do!

Not ready for clapping, singing, and declaring just yet? No problem. Pray. Bring in Angels, God, Jesus, the saints, Light Beings, or any of your protectors and guides to guard and keep your space sacred.

Play upbeat music. Have om chanting or sacred solfeggio frequencies playing softly in the background.

Maintenance

Be sure to smudge and clear anything that you bring into your home. Be especially mindful of used furniture, cars, and jewelry. All these items have imprinted energy from their previous owners and situations. Energy that may not be at the level of love, light, health, and happiness you wish to maintain in your home.

If you are considering a new home, property, or apartment, take some time and research the land. There are just some properties that are never going to be hospitable to peace and joy no matter how much you smudge! Best to take a pass on those spots.

Do a walk through by yourself. Take your time. Feel. How is the energy? Don't be self-conscious. You are the one who will need to live here. It's worth 20 minutes doing a *feel* of the place. It's much easier to find an energetically clear building then to get an energetically dirty building clear.

Smudge or clear your space as needed. I'm often asked, "How often do I need to clear and smudge?"

The answer is as often as needed! Just like dusting, when it's time, you know it.

Cautions

Beyond the obvious cautions when using fire and burning objects, be careful if you have, or suspect you have, *uninvited guests* that are reluctant to leave your space. Provoking negative spirits will not normally have a positive outcome from your efforts to clear them. You'll have better results by filling the area with light and love than banishing and expelling.

Low-frequency entities are not comfortable in high-frequency spaces. They will often leave on their own if you get and keep the frequencies high.

Most importantly, you do not have the authority to send something or someone to hell, or whatever you may call it in your tradition. That will backfire on you. Don't do it!

You can send something or someone back to source or back to where it is from. You can and should love it back into perfection. Trust me—that is a much better choice.

Be sure to enjoy the other publications and videos from Susan K. Edwards. NiceRockShop.com

ADOBE STOCK

Certain photographs used in this book have been licensed from Adobe Stock.

These photographs are protected by copyright law. Resale or use of any photos used in this book is prohibited.

Photographs © / Adobe Stock

Manufactured by Amazon.ca
Bolton, ON